baya

S0-AIH-181

BIAS IN AMERICA

# Black
# IN AMERICA

Hal Marcovitz

ReferencePoint
Press

San Diego, CA

© 2021 ReferencePoint Press, Inc.
Printed in the United States

**For more information, contact:**
ReferencePoint Press, Inc.
PO Box 27779
San Diego, CA 92198
www.ReferencePointPress.com

LIBRARY OF CONGRESS CATALOGING-IN-PUBLICATION DATA

Names: Marcovitz, Hal, author.
Title: Black in America / by Hal Marcovitz.
Description: San Diego, CA : ReferencePoint Press, Inc., 2021. | Series: Bias in America | Includes bibliographical references and index.
Identifiers: LCCN 2020011941 (print) | LCCN 2020011942 (ebook) | ISBN 9781682828915 (library binding) | ISBN 9781682828922 (ebook)
Subjects: LCSH: Racism--United States--History. | United States--Race relations--History. | African Americans--Social conditions--21st century. | Racial profiling in law enforcement--United States. | Police brutality--United States.
Classification: LCC E185.615 .M287 2021 (print) | LCC E185.615 (ebook) | DDC 305.896/073--dc23
LC record available at https://lccn.loc.gov/2020011941
LC ebook record available at https://lccn.loc.gov/2020011942

# CONTENTS

# Some Ugly Truths

Dante Petty, his wife, and their young daughter came home one evening to their Grapevine, Texas, apartment to find a cruel message blocking their way. Someone had strapped a noose around the neck of an African American doll and hung it in the doorway leading up to the Petty apartment.

The Pettys are African American. During the Jim Crow era in the South, dating from the period following the Civil War to the middle of the twentieth century, many racist mobs kidnapped innocent black people and murdered them by lynching—hanging them from trees. The doll hanging in front of the Pettys' apartment was intended to serve as a stark message to the young family—that they were not welcome in their apartment complex.

Dante Petty feared for the safety of his family. He installed a surveillance camera outside his apartment. Soon, the camera caught one of Petty's neighbors, Glenn Halfin, hanging the doll again. Petty turned the surveillance video over to police, who soon arrested Halfin, a sixty-four-year-old white man, charging him with harassing the Petty family. "No one should be afraid to go home at night," said US Attorney Erin Nealy Cox at the time of Halfin's arrest in December 2017. "Our community will not tolerate crimes of intimidation or bigotry, and my office will continue to prosecute all those who persecute others based on their race, color, ethnicity, or religious beliefs."[1]

## Racial Bias in American Life

Although Cox's office was quick to prosecute Halfin, the incident nevertheless illustrates how racial bias against African Americans remains part of the fabric of American life, four hundred years after the first African slaves stepped off a ship docking near Jamestown, Virginia. Since then, Americans have fought a Civil War, enacted amendments to the US Constitution, and made numerous changes to other laws, all in the interest of treating everyone equally. And yet, racial bias continues to exist in American life.

And cases of bias like the incident in Grapevine occur even though the US Congress has passed tough laws against hate crimes—crimes that are inflicted on people solely because of their race, religious faith, ethnicity, or gender identity. According to the Federal Bureau of Investigation, in 2018—the last year for which statistics are available—police investigated 7,120 hate crimes in US communities. The incident involving the Petty family served

Americans have fought a Civil War (pictured is the Battle of Shiloh, which took place in Tennessee in 1862), enacted amendments to the US Constitution, and have made numerous changes to other laws, all in the interest of treating everyone equally. And yet, racial bias continues to exist in American life.

as a typical example. According to court records, "Halfin [hung the doll] knowing that this display would be particularly intimidating for the family who had a young daughter."[2] In 2018, Halfin pleaded guilty to committing a hate crime against the Petty family. He was sentenced to a year in jail.

The act of terrorizing the Petty family by lynching a black doll in front of their apartment illustrates a very blatant and hostile form of racial bias. But bias can be found in other forms as well. Although lynch mobs of the Jim Crow era are no longer the norm, black people often face violent attacks simply because they are black. Comedians no longer wear blackface makeup and portray African Americans as comical characters, but racially insensitive humor can be heard in barrooms across America. Racist graffiti is still found on city walls. Many racists find an outlet for their hatred on social media.

## Subtle Forms of Bias

But there are other, more subtle forms of racial bias. The National Football League (NFL) provides one such example. The NFL is dominated by black players—some 70 percent of the athletes in the league are African American. But in 2020, only three of the league's thirty-two head coaches were black. In fact, the NFL lacks diversity among one of its most important categories of employment despite the adoption of the so-called Rooney Rule in 2003. The rule, spearheaded by then–Pittsburgh Steelers owner Art Rooney, requires NFL teams to interview minority candidates whenever they have head coaching vacancies. So even though team owners and their subordinates are required to interview black candidates for the jobs, in truth the black candidates are rarely awarded the positions.

"We're celebrating the 100th anniversary of the NFL (in 2020), yet we have only three head coaches of color," said Rod Graves, a former league official. "For all the hoopla that football has become in this country, that kind of progress, or lack of, is shameful."[3] In early 2020, shortly before the Super Bowl, NFL commissioner Roger Goodell acknowledged that the Rooney Rule has been ineffective. He announced plans to reevaluate the league's policies governing minority hiring to find ways for more African Americans to obtain head coaching jobs. "Clearly, we are not where we want to be on this level,"[4] Goodell said.

> "We're celebrating the 100th anniversary of the NFL (in 2020), yet we have only three head coaches of color."[3]
>
> —Rod Graves, former NFL official

Still, as the NFL's dismal record on hiring black head coaches illustrates, racial bias continues to rear its ugly head in America. More than four hundred years since they were brought to American shores as slaves, black people continue to find themselves facing racial bias in the schools they attend, in the places they shop, and even on the streets where they walk and drive. And bias exists as well in places like professional football—a slice of American culture where black participants may have believed they had long ago won acceptance.

# CHAPTER ONE

# Struggles Against Racism

Hampton, Virginia, is a bustling community with a population of more than one hundred thousand people. Built on the shores of the Chesapeake Bay, Hampton features all the elements of a typical small American city: shopping malls, industrial parks, and housing developments fill the landscape. Each summer, baseball fans head over to Hampton's War Memorial Stadium, home of the Peninsula Pilots, a minor league team that has sent several players into the Major Leagues. Among those players is Ryan Zimmerman, who played first base for the Washington Nationals during the team's World Series–winning season of 2019.

Long before Zimmerman was fielding ground balls for the Peninsula Pilots, Hampton was known for a much sadder chapter of American history. Four centuries ago, Hampton was known as Point-Comfort. In 1607, colonists from England landed in Virginia to establish the first American colony in nearby Jamestown. In 1619, many of those colonists gathered at Point-Comfort to greet the arrival of an English ship, the *White Lion*. On board were some twenty young men and women captured by slave traders in what was then known as the Kingdom of Ndongo—today, the African nation of Angola.

The colonists were happy to accept the slaves—their labor was needed in the farm fields that colonists had established in Jamestown. In exchange for the slaves, the colonists paid the captain of the *White Lion* with food and other supplies. The slaves were given new names by their owners, among them Anthony, Isabela, William, Angela, Frances, Margaret, John, and Edward. They were put to work in the fields as well as the homes of their new owners. And so began the era of slavery in America—a dark and unmistakably contrary chapter in a nation founded more than 150 years later on the principles of equality, liberty, and the pursuit of happiness for all. Says Glenn C. Loury, a professor of social sciences at Brown University in Rhode Island, quoting Abraham Lincoln, "The United States of America, 'a new nation, conceived in liberty and dedicated to the proposition that all men are created equal,' began as a slave society. What can rightly be called the 'original sin,' slavery has left an indelible imprint on our nation's soul."[5]

> "The United States of America, 'a new nation, conceived in liberty and dedicated to the proposition that all men are created equal,' began as a slave society."[5]
>
> —Glenn C. Loury, Brown University social sciences professor

*In the early colonial period, colonists at Jamestown (pictured) were happy to accept African slaves from traders to work their farms. This was the beginning of the era of slavery in America.*

# Three-Fifths Compromise

By 1776, some 286,000 Africans had been captured in their homeland, shipped across the Atlantic Ocean, and sold into slavery in America. That was the year the American colonies rebelled against Great Britain—a conflict born among colonists who fought for self-determination, insisting that no foreign king should hold power over their lives. The American Revolution ended in 1783 with Great Britain granting independence to the colonies. In 1789, delegates meeting in Philadelphia ratified the US Constitution, the laws that would govern the new nation. The preamble to the Constitution reads: "We the People of the United States, in Order to form a more perfect Union, establish Justice, insure domestic Tranquility, provide for the common defense, promote the general Welfare, and secure the Blessings of Liberty to ourselves and our Posterity, do ordain and establish this Constitution for the United States of America."

These were noble and important words, but they didn't apply to everyone. If you were a black slave living in the South, the Constitution did not apply to you. In fact, the Constitution didn't even treat the slaves as people. A question that vexed the delegates to the Constitutional Convention was how to ensure that the states were properly represented in the new US Congress. It was decided that the states would be split into congressional districts with the states with larger populations receiving more congressional districts and, therefore, more members in the House of Representatives. But since slaves weren't citizens, the states from the South balked at this plan. By now, there were more than 340,000 slaves working on southern plantations. The southern delegates demanded they receive representation in Congress reflecting the number of slaves living on their plantations—although, of course, slaves had no freedoms.

And so the delegates struck what was known as the "three-fifths compromise." For purposes of representation in Congress, each slave would count as three-fifths of a person, thereby enhancing southern representation in Congress without granting slaves any of the benefits the Congress intended to enact for all other Americans. John Jay, who served as the first chief justice of the United States, saw through the phoniness of the three-fifths compromise, writing, "It is much to be wished that slavery may be abolished. The honour of the States, as well as justice and humanity, in my opinion, loudly call upon them to emancipate these unhappy people. To contend for our own liberty, and to deny that blessing to others, involves an inconsistency not to be excused."[6]

> "The honour of the States, as well as justice and humanity, in my opinion, loudly call upon them to emancipate these unhappy people."[6]
>
> —John Jay, first chief justice of the United States

John Jay (pictured), who served as the first chief justice of the United States, used his influence to ban slavery in his home state of New York.

## The Slave Auction

Jay used his influence to ban slavery in his home state of New York. Other northern states took similar action, but states in the South refused to outlaw slavery. By now, cotton was the predominant crop in the South, and slaves were vitally needed to grow and harvest the crop. By the 1860s, some 4 million slaves were toiling on southern plantations. In 1891, the former slave Harriet Ann Jacobs published her autobiography, describing what life was like for black slaves on a southern plantation. Jacobs recalled that in the South, New Year's Day was typically the day of the annual slave auction—when plantation owners met in the town square to buy and sell slaves among themselves. She wrote,

"If a slave is unwilling to go with his new master, he is whipped, or locked up in jail, until he consents to go, and promises not to run away during the year."[7]

—Harriet Ann Jacobs, former slave

If a slave is unwilling to go with his new master, he is whipped, or locked up in jail, until he consents to go, and promises not to run away during the year. Should he chance to change his mind, thinking it justifiable to violate an extorted promise, woe unto him if he is caught! The whip is used till the blood flows at his feet; and his stiffened limbs are put in chains, to be dragged in the field for days and days. . . .

On one of these days I saw a slave mother lead seven children to the auction-block. She knew that some of them would be taken from her; but they took all. The children were sold to a slave-trader, and their mother was bought by a man in her own town. Before night her children were all far away. She begged the trader to tell where he intended to take them; this he refused to do. How could he, when he would sell them one by one to wherever he could command the highest price?[7]

In the northern states, there had been a growing movement since the founding of the nation contending that slavery was

# Blackface Makeup and Jim Crow

The term "Jim Crow" has long been applied to an era of American life in which black citizens were denied basic rights. During the era of segregation in the South, many states adopted Jim Crow laws, banning black citizens from entering whites-only restaurants, theaters, restrooms, railroad cars, and similar places.

The term "Jim Crow" was first used in the 1830s and 1840s by a white entertainer, Thomas Dartmouth Rice, who traveled the country performing a song and dance act. Rice dressed as a field slave and wore blackface makeup. He named his buffoonish character "Jim Crow."

In modern times, wearing blackface makeup is regarded as racially insensitive, but cases still surface from time to time. In 2019, thirty-five-year-old photographs of Virginia governor Ralph Northam surfaced showing Northam—then a medical student—wearing blackface makeup while participating in a dance contest. (He was portraying African American pop star Michael Jackson.) Some Virginia political leaders demanded Northam resign, but he refused. Many African American political leaders supported Northam during the controversy, agreeing that a foolish act by a student thirty-five years earlier should be forgiven.

Meanwhile, in 2020 two participants in Philadelphia's annual New Year's Day Mummers Parade were found to be wearing blackface. After the parade, Philadelphia mayor James Kenney demanded that Mummers officials ban blackface makeup or he would cancel the 2021 parade. Meanwhile, after the parade, members of the Philadelphia City Council introduced a bill that would make it illegal to wear blackface makeup in the parade. Mummers officials said they supported the bill.

wrong and should be abolished. In the early 1800s an abolitionist movement commenced. Over the next few decades, many slaves were able to escape and find refuge in the northern states. They received help from free blacks and sympathetic white people participating in a secretive network known as the Underground Railroad.

# Freeing the Slaves

Some abolitionists were not satisfied with merely smuggling slaves to the North, insisting that an armed slave rebellion against the slave owners was the only way to end slavery. In 1859, the radical abolitionist John Brown led an attack on a US Army arsenal in Harper's Ferry, Virginia, with the plan to obtain weapons and arm slaves so they could rise up against their masters. The raid failed. Brown and his men were captured and executed by hanging on December 1, 1859.

Still, the incident helped stoke fear among southerners, who were now convinced that the abolitionist movement in the North aimed to use force to free the slaves. In 1860, Abraham Lincoln was elected president. Lincoln believed slavery was morally wrong and sympathized with the abolitionist movement. Many southern whites believed he represented a danger to their way of life and some southern states began to secede from, or drop out of, the United States. On April 12, 1861—thirty-nine days after Lincoln was inaugurated as president—the first shots were fired at Fort Sumter in South Carolina between US forces and secessionist militias, touching off the Civil War. Eventually, thirteen states seceded from the union. They were known as the Confederate States of America, or simply the Confederacy.

The war continued for four years and produced a staggering death toll: an estimated 360,000 Union soldiers lost their lives, while 258,000 Confederate soldiers were killed before the South finally surrendered. Given that the entire population of the country at the time was about 31 million people, it means that about 2 percent of American citizens lost their lives in the war. Of course, tens of thousands of other soldiers on both sides returned home with devastating wounds such as the loss of arms and legs.

But the Union victory ensured the freedom of the slaves. In 1862, Lincoln had issued the Emancipation Proclamation, freeing all American slaves—although his order was ignored in the Southern states. But following the war, in 1865, Congress adopted and the state legislatures ratified the Thirteenth Amendment to the

US Constitution, officially making it unlawful to hold slaves in the United States. Over the next five years, two more constitutional amendments were passed: the Fourteenth Amendment, ensuring that all US citizens, regardless of race, enjoyed equal protection under the law, and the Fifteenth Amendment, making it illegal to deny citizens the right to vote based on their race.

## Jim Crow Laws

Now free and believing themselves to enjoy protections under the US Constitution, the new citizens of America hardly found the life that they had been promised. Over the next several decades, embittered whites controlling the state governments in the South enacted a series of Jim Crow laws, essentially barring black people from the same rights enjoyed by white citizens. Black students could not attend the same schools as white students. Railroad trains had "Whites Only" and "Colored Only" cars. Black people could not eat in restaurants or go to theaters that catered to white patrons. Public restrooms and water fountains were segregated.

*Police stand over the body of a young African American man who was stoned to death by a group of white men in 1919. Between 1882 and 1968 it is estimated that 4,743 black Americans were killed by whites.*

Hotels in the South did not accept black guests. Many of these laws endured well into the twentieth century. Recalls Charles Gratton, who grew up in the 1930s in the Norwood neighborhood of Birmingham, Alabama:

> I can remember very close in my mind [times] when my mother would send me to this grocery store that was approximately a mile away, which was the only grocery store in Norwood. She would give me instructions before I'd leave home and tell me, "Son, now you go on up to this store and get this or that for me. If you pass any white people on your way, you get off the sidewalk. Give them the sidewalk. You move over. Don't challenge white people." So I was just brought up in that environment.

> They also had a park. It was about a block from where I was born and raised and where I lived, and it was known as the white people's park. They had a tennis court there and nice park trees, and blacks [were not] allowed in that park. I mean we just couldn't go there. You know, it's just one of those things."[8]

Moreover, black citizens often found themselves victims of mob rule. Following the Civil War, the white supremacist group known as the Ku Klux Klan grew in membership. The group, initially composed of Confederate Army veterans, terrorized black people—kidnapping them off the streets, then murdering them through the horrific act of lynching. And the terror continued for over a century. According to the civil rights group the National Association for the Advancement of Colored People (NAACP), 4,743 black Americans lost their lives in lynchings between 1882 and 1968.

An 1899 newspaper article described a typical case in Palmetto, Georgia. It told of a black man, Lije Strickland, who was kidnapped by a lynch mob and accused of the murder of a white man named Alfred Cranford. The US Constitution guaranteed Strickland equal protection under the law, including the right to due process—meaning the right to be tried fairly in a court of law by a judge and jury. The mob, however, would have none of that. Reported the newspaper,

> Before being lynched, Strickland was given a chance to confess to the misdeeds of which the mob supposed him to be guilty, but he protested his innocence to the last. Three times, the noose was placed around his neck and the [black man] was drawn up off the ground; three times he was let down with a warning that death was in store for him, should he fail to confess his complicity in the Cranford murder. Three times Strickland proclaimed his innocence, until weary of useless torturing, the mob pulled on the rope and tied the end around the slender trunk of the persimmon tree. Not a shot was fired. Strickland was strangled to death.[9]

## Era of Desegregation

By the 1940s, great strides were finally being made to outlaw the types of treatment that black people had been forced to accept since gaining their freedom at the end of the Civil War. In 1947, Jackie Robinson led the integration of professional sports when the Brooklyn Dodgers signed him to a contract. Following the outbreak of the Korean War in 1950, the US armed forces were desegregated—meaning soldiers of all races served beside one another in the conflict. In all previous wars, black soldiers were restricted to service in black-only units. In 1954, the US Supreme Court outlawed segregated schools in the case known as *Brown v. Board of Education*. In 1955, an African American woman, Rosa Parks, refused to give up her seat to a white man

"Before being lynched, Strickland was given a chance to confess to the misdeeds of which the mob supposed him to be guilty, but he protested his innocence to the last."[9]

—Georgia newspaper report of the 1899 lynching of Lije Strickland

# The US Supreme Court and Racial Equality

The US Supreme Court has issued many rulings that have helped ensure people of all races are treated equally. One of the most notable rulings is from the 1954 case of *Brown v. Board of Education*. In that case, the justices ruled unanimously that racial segregation of children in public schools is unconstitutional.

But the Supreme Court has also gotten things wrong. The *Brown v. Board of Education* ruling overturned an earlier high court decision. That case grew out of a lawsuit filed by Homer Plessy, a black man who was barred access to a whites-only railroad car. In 1896 the justices ruled in *Plessy v. Ferguson* that as long as the blacks-only car provided the same service to Plessy, there was nothing wrong with the railroad's policy of separating the races. In other words, the court ruled that the notion of "separate but equal" was constitutional, not only for railroad cars but for schools and other places in American society.

The Supreme Court's 8–1 ruling upheld the practice of segregation. The lone dissenting vote was cast by Justice John Marshall Harlan, a former slaveholder from Kentucky who, since the Civil War, established himself as a vocal advocate for equality. In his dissenting opinion, Harlan wrote, "The arbitrary separation of citizens on the basis of race while they are on a public highway is a badge of servitude wholly inconsistent with the civil freedom and the equality before the law established by the Constitution. It cannot be justified upon any legal grounds."

Quoted in History.com, "Plessy v. Ferguson," February 21, 2020. www.history.com.

on a bus in Montgomery, Alabama. She was arrested, sparking the Montgomery Bus Boycott. This was a citywide campaign, led by the Reverend Dr. Martin Luther King Jr., in which black people refused to ride city buses. Their refusal to ride the buses led to the near-bankruptcy of the bus company and an eventual court decision finding that racial segregation of public transit was unconstitutional. And in 1964, Congress passed the US Civil Rights Act mandating the desegregation of all American institutions.

By the 1960s, African American political leaders found they could be taken seriously not only when they ran for office representing constituencies of predominantly black voters but more broadly as well. In 1966, Edward Brooke of Massachusetts became the first African American elected to the US Senate. And, in 1990, Douglas Wilder of Virginia became the nation's first black to be elected governor.

On January 20, 2009, an African American, Barack Obama, raised his hand to take the oath of office as the forty-fourth president of the United States. His swearing-in ceremony occurred 390 years after the first black slaves arrived in Port-Comfort. Many believed that America had finally made the transition to a society of complete inclusion. Certainly, they insisted, any society that would elect a black candidate to the presidency had finally put its long and sordid history of racism and bias to rest. Shortly after Obama's election, political commentator Dinesh D'Souza said, "There could not be a better sign that America has left behind its racist past. We are now approaching what may be termed the end of racism."[10]

But D'Souza and other observers were wrong. Despite the election of a black president in 2008, as well as Obama's reelection in 2012, bias against black citizens remains a very real part of life in twenty-first-century America. All too often, black people find themselves frozen out of the rights and opportunities guaranteed to all Americans. And in many cases, they are still subjected to racially motivated harassment and violence.

# Victimized by Police

Michael Brown would never have been regarded as an angel. On the morning of August 9, 2014, Brown, an eighteen-year-old black man from Ferguson, Missouri, entered a convenience store in the St. Louis suburb, where he is alleged to have shoplifted a package of small cigars. Moreover, a security camera captured the image of Brown shoving a clerk on his way out of the store.

A few minutes later, as Brown and another young black man, twenty-two-year-old Dorian Johnson, walked down the center of Canfield Drive in Ferguson, a police cruiser pulled alongside of them. The officer, Darren Wilson, had been summoned to the scene by the Ferguson police dispatcher, who had reported a theft in progress at the convenience store. Wilson, who is white, suspected Brown and Johnson of participating in the theft.

Wilson told Brown and Johnson to get out of the street and use the sidewalk. According to Wilson, as he tried to open the door of his cruiser Brown threw a punch at him and reached for his gun. A struggle ensued. Wilson was able to wrestle the gun away from Brown and fire two shots, one of which hit Brown in the hand. Brown then ran away. Wilson gave chase. Suddenly, Wilson said, Brown turned and charged toward him. Wilson fired his gun again—

releasing twelve shots at Brown, six of which hit the young man. Two shots struck Brown in the head, killing him instantly. Later, when investigators interviewed witnesses, they were told a much different story: that Brown had raised his hands in an effort to surrender to Wilson, but the police officer nevertheless fired at the unarmed man.

Brown's death was not a unique circumstance. For decades, black people—particularly young black men—have found themselves under suspicion by police even though they may be entirely innocent. And in many cases, police have resorted to violent means to apprehend these black suspects, often shooting them with little or no provocation.

That Brown was suspected of shoplifting—a minor crime that rarely results in jail time—is undisputed. The outcome of this incident is what led to a wave of angry protest. Most

*A protester holds up a sign in memory of eighteen-year-old Michael Brown. In 2014, Brown was shot and killed by a white police officer even though witnesses say that Brown tried to surrender.*

" it's so beautiful, yet so painful to be BLACK"
— sandro Bland.

Mike Brown
REST IN PEACE

D NOT FORGET Y

people would agree that losing one's life over some stolen cigars is hardly a fitting punishment. Making matters worse, the Brown shooting is not an isolated event. Other police shootings involving unarmed black men have occurred in the years since the Brown incident. Says Jennifer Cobbina, a professor at the Michigan State University School of Criminal Justice,

> These killings . . . are hardly outliers. Rather, they are examples of racial hostility, racial bias, legalized racial subordination, and a normative police practice that targets black individuals. But the issue of racially motivated police killings is not simply a product of individual discriminatory police officers. It is the result of deep historical forces that follow a pattern of social control over black people that is entwined in the very fabric of the United States.[11]

## Young Black Men Are Often Victims

Police shootings in America are not uncommon. According to the science journal *Nature*, police in America fire fatal shots at suspects about three times a day. Moreover, studies have shown that in American communities, black people are fatally targeted by police far more often than white people.

For example, statistics compiled by the group Mapping Police Violence reported that of the 1,143 Americans who were killed in police shootings in 2018, 23 percent were black, even though black people make up just 13 percent of the American population. Moreover, the group reported that 21 percent of black victims of fatal police shootings were unarmed, compared to 14 percent of white victims.

Those are national statistics, but when the group looked at large cities—places

"These killings . . . are hardly outliers. Rather, they are examples of racial hostility, racial bias, legalized racial subordination, and a normative police practice that targets black individuals."[11]

—Jennifer Cobbina, professor at the Michigan State University School of Criminal Justice

# Police Killings of African American Men

The rate of police killings of African American men exceeds the US murder rate in eight big-city police departments. This is the finding of the group Mapping Police Violence, which compiled statistics from the nation's one hundred largest city police departments for the years 2013 to 2019. The study found that black men are in the most danger of being shot by police in Reno, Nevada; Oklahoma City, Oklahoma; and Santa Ana, California.

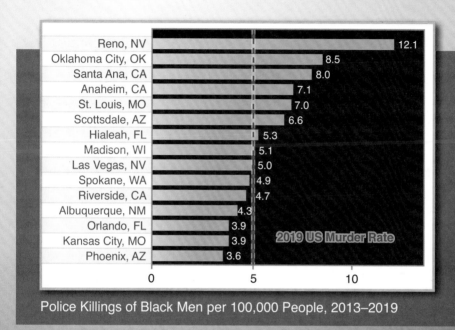

| City | Rate |
|------|------|
| Reno, NV | 12.1 |
| Oklahoma City, OK | 8.5 |
| Santa Ana, CA | 8.0 |
| Anaheim, CA | 7.1 |
| St. Louis, MO | 7.0 |
| Scottsdale, AZ | 6.6 |
| Hialeah, FL | 5.3 |
| Madison, WI | 5.1 |
| Las Vegas, NV | 5.0 |
| Spokane, WA | 4.9 |
| Riverside, CA | 4.7 |
| Albuquerque, NM | 4.3 |
| Orlando, FL | 3.9 |
| Kansas City, MO | 3.9 |
| Phoenix, AZ | 3.6 |

2019 US Murder Rate

Police Killings of Black Men per 100,000 People, 2013–2019

Source: Mapping Police Violence, April 1, 2020. https://mappingpoliceviolence.org.

which typically feature large concentrations of black residents—the numbers show an even greater prominence of black victims. In the one hundred largest American cities, the group found, black people accounted for 38 percent of the victims of police shootings, even though they represented just 21 percent of the populations in those cities. In other words, in the nation's largest cities, black people are killed at nearly twice the rate of nonblack people in police shootings as nonblack people.

A separate study, published in 2019 in the journal *Proceedings of the National Academy of Sciences*, found that one in one thousand African American boys and men will die in a police shooting. "That 1-in-1,000 number struck us as quite high," said study leader Frank Edwards, a sociologist at Rutgers University in New Jersey. "That's better odds of being killed by police than you have of winning a lot of scratch-off lottery games."[12] In fact, the study found, black men face a higher risk of dying from being shot by police officers than they do from succumbing to such diseases as diabetes, pneumonia, and the flu.

The study found that young black men are two and a half times more likely to be shot by police than young men of other races. Moreover, study findings show that police shootings are the cause of death for 1.6 percent of all young black men between the ages of twenty and twenty-four. "That's quite meaningful," said Justin Feldman, a physician at the New York University School of Medicine who studies causes of death among social classes. "If it's not you being killed by police, it's someone you know or someone in your community."[13]

## Lack of Higher Education a Factor

Sociologists and other scholars have studied why police officers are more likely to shoot black people, and many agree with Cobbina—that the reason can be traced to America's racist past. As far back as 1944, the topic of police violence against black people raised the interest of Swedish sociologist Gunnar Myrdal, who specifically studied police violence against black people in southern states. He wrote, "The average southern policeman is a promoted white with a legal sanction to use a weapon. His social heritage has taught him to despise the [blacks], and he has had little education which could have changed him. . . . The result is that probably no group of whites in America have a lower opinion and are more fixed in their views than southern policemen."[14]

Myrdal studied the issue more than seventy-five years ago, but modern scholars find that attitudes in many twenty-first-century police departments aren't that much different than they were in the 1940s. Write sociologists Cassandra Chaney and Ray V. Robertson, "The current research does corroborate [Myrdal's] obser-

## The Talk

Black parents often find it necessary to have a discussion with their children—particularly their sons—on how to respond if they are approached by white police officers. Black parents have taken to calling this conversation "The Talk."

Says Judy Belk, the mother of two African American sons,

> You know, the [talk] where we remind our young men and women that when they leave the safety of their homes, they have to keep their guard up, mouths shut, and hands on the wheel in even the most casual encounters with law enforcement. It's an unfair but necessary burden we carry in the black community, one we reluctantly pass down to our children if we want to keep them alive and safe.

In recent years, civil rights organizations and other groups have held workshops in black communities advising parents on how to have this conversation with their children. Among these groups are the Washington, DC–based Jack and Jill of America, the New York City–based All Stars Project Inc., and the Alexandria, Virginia–based National Organization of Black Law Enforcement Executives (NOBLE). Speaking in 2019, Perry Tarrant, the assistant police chief in Seattle, Washington, said, "NOBLE has been inundated with a number of requests for this program. We've done it somewhere in the thousands, I believe somewhere around 2,000 times over, just within the last three years."

Judy Belk, "Opinion: As a Black Parent, I Need to Update 'The Talk' I Have with My Kids About Police," *Los Angeles Times*, November 3, 2019. www.latimes.com.

Quoted in Candace Smith and Alexa Valiente, "Workshops Help Parents Have 'The Talk' with Kids on What It Means to Be Black in the US," ABC News, January 16, 2018. https://abcnews.go.com.

vations that less educated police officers tend to be the most aggressive and have the most formal complaints filed against them when compared to their more educated counterparts."[15]

According to the US Bureau of Labor Statistics, most police departments in the United States require job candidates to be no more than high school graduates or, if they have dropped out of high school, to have earned a General Equivalency Diploma (GED). However, many four-year colleges as well as two-year community colleges offer degrees in law enforcement, and candidates with college degrees are often given preference for jobs with police departments. Still, according to the National Police Foundation, an Arlington, Virginia, group that studies trends in law enforcement, about half of American police officers lack degrees from either four-year or two-year colleges. In 2014, one of those officers who lacked post-high-school education was Darren Wilson, the Ferguson police officer who shot Michael Brown.

## Willing to Draw Their Weapons

While the educational backgrounds of the officers may be one factor in why police are more likely to shoot blacks than whites, the overriding factor in why black people are targeted so often by police is racial bias. A 2005 study at Florida State University looked at how police respond to suspicious persons. Fifty police officers participated in the study: 84 percent were white, 10 per-

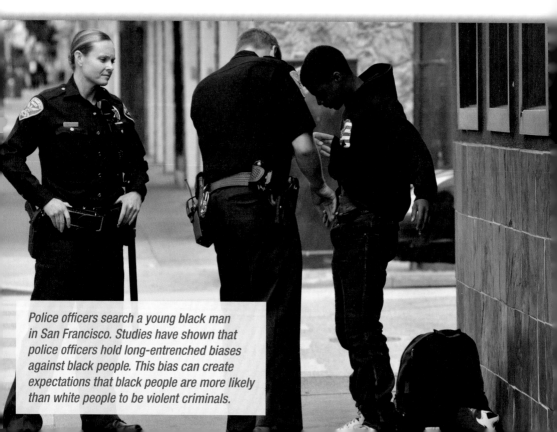

Police officers search a young black man in San Francisco. Studies have shown that police officers hold long-entrenched biases against black people. This bias can create expectations that black people are more likely than white people to be violent criminals.

cent were black, and the remainder were Native American and Hispanic. The officers were shown computer simulations of people and were told some of them are carrying guns. Others carried nonthreatening objects, such as wallets or cell phones. The police officers were instructed to press a key on their keyboards to simulate firing their weapons at people whom they regarded as dangerous—in other words, suspects armed with guns.

The results were clear: The police officers who participated in the study were far more likely to fire their weapons at black men—even those carrying cell phones or wallets—than they were at white individuals. "The officers were . . . more likely to mistakenly shoot unarmed black suspects than unarmed white suspects," wrote psychologists E. Ashby Plant and B. Michelle Peruche, authors of the study. "These findings are troubling because racial biases in officers' response to criminal suspects could have tragic implications if such biases generalize to real-life decisions."[16]

"The officers were . . . more likely to mistakenly shoot unarmed black suspects than unarmed white suspects."[16]

—E. Ashby Plant and B. Michelle Peruche, psychologists

In their study, Plant and Peruche concluded that police officers hold long-entrenched biases against black people—that they consider them aggressive and their behavior often criminal. Wrote Plant and Peruche, "This stereotype may create expectations that black people, and particularly black men, are more likely than white people to be violent criminals, which may lead to racially biased interpretations of suspects' behavior."[17]

## Explicit Racial Bias in Ferguson

In the Ferguson case, Wilson insisted that his decision to shoot Brown was not racially motivated—that he felt his life was in danger when Brown charged him. In fact, Wilson said, when he joined the Ferguson police he realized that as a white man he would have trouble relating to the mostly black residents of the Missouri community, and he sought counsel from other police officers who helped him find common ground with the black citizens. Wilson said he thought he was making progress when the Brown shooting occurred. "I liked the black community," he said. "I had fun there. . . . There's people who will just crack you up."[18]

Four months after the shooting of Brown, Wilson was exonerated of any wrongdoing. Prosecutors presented the case to a grand jury, an investigative body composed of citizens chosen to hear the evidence. After examining the evidence and hearing testimony from witnesses, the grand jury decided not to charge Wilson with a crime. Wilson did, however, resign from the Ferguson Police Department.

In March 2015, the US Justice Department issued its own report on the shooting of Brown, leveling heavy criticism at the Ferguson police—finding the department rife with racial bias toward black citizens. Among the findings of the report: almost 90 percent of unnecessary force was directed at African Americans; the use of police dogs was exclusively reserved for African Americans; and 90 percent of stops and arrests for reasons as minor as jaywalking—illegally walking in streets—involved black citizens. In announcing the findings of the Justice Department report, US Attorney General Eric Holder said, "These policing practices disproportionately harm African American residents. In fact, our review of the evidence found no alternative explanation for the disproportionate impact on African American residents other than implicit and explicit racial bias."[19]

> "I liked the black community. I had fun there."[18]
>
> —Darren Wilson, former Ferguson police officer

## Police Officers Face Justice

Brown was certainly not the first African American to be the victim of excessive police force. Nor was he the last. After Brown's death, other members of black communities—frequently young men—have been killed by police. As with Wilson, some of those police officers have been exonerated after investigations into the circumstances surrounding their cases. In other instances, however, prosecutors have found reason to criminally charge the police officers who fired the fatal shots.

## State Police Lack Records on Racial Makup

State police departments—in which officers are empowered to patrol in any community in their home state—are maintained by forty-nine state governments in the United States (Hawaii does not maintain a state police department). Statistics released in 2019 reflect how closely those forty-nine state police departments monitor racial bias among their officers.

According to an investigation by the group Spotlight, which is supported by numerous news organizations, eleven state police departments do not keep statistics on the race or ethnicity of suspects who are arrested or detained, or the motorists who are issued traffic citations. Those states are Idaho, New Mexico, South Dakota, Minnesota, Arkansas, Louisiana, Alabama, West Virginia, Pennsylvania, Maine, and New Hampshire.

Civil rights activists believe police agencies should collect data on the race of people who come into contact with officers. They contend the availability of such statistics would help identify racial bias in those departments. "It makes it look like you either don't care about disparities or you are trying to hide what the data shows," said Christy Lopez, a professor at Georgetown University School of Law in Washington, DC.

Quoted in Angela Couloumbis and Daniel Simmons-Ritchie, "Collection of Race Data Was Halted in 2012," September 22, 2019, *Philadelphia Inquirer*, p. A1.

In 2017, former North Charleston, South Carolina, police officer Michael Slager was sentenced to twenty years in a federal prison for shooting Walter Scott, a fifty-year-old black man, two years earlier. Slager had stopped Scott's vehicle because it had a broken brake light. As Slager approached Scott's vehicle, Scott got out of his car and started running away. A video recorded by a witness with a cell phone showed Slager draw his gun and fire at the fleeing man. Five bullets struck Scott in the back, killing him instantly. In sentencing Slager, US district judge David Norton said, "[Slager] acted out of malice and forethought, shooting dead an unarmed and fleeing Walter Scott. Slager's actions were disproportional to Scott's misconduct."[20]

Another police officer who was convicted in the shooting death of a black man was Dallas, Texas, officer Amber Guyger. In 2018, Guyger returned to her apartment after a late shift to discover a black man inside. She quickly drew her gun and fired, killing twenty-six-year-old accountant Botham Jean. As it turned out, Guyger hadn't entered her apartment—she had mistakenly entered Jean's apartment and, believing the occupant to be a burglar, drew her gun and fired a fatal shot. In 2019, Guyger was convicted on a charge of murder and sentenced to ten years in prison.

Other police officers have been similarly charged but ultimately acquitted. In 2016, Tulsa, Oklahoma, police officer Betty Shelby was charged in the fatal shooting of Terence Crutcher, a forty-year-old unarmed black man. Shelby testified during her trial that she shot Crutcher after he ignored her commands and reached into his car for what she believed was a gun. She was found not guilty by a jury.

In 2018, Pittsburgh, Pennsylvania, police officer Michael Rosfeld was also found not guilty by a jury after he was charged in the fatal shooting of Antwon Rose II, an unarmed black teenager. Rosfeld said he had stopped Rose's vehicle because it matched the description of a car that was involved in an earlier shooting. When Rose brought his car to a stop, he jumped out and ran from the scene. Rosfeld fired his gun at the fleeing seventeen-year-old youth, hitting him three times. The jury in the Rosfeld case deliberated for four hours before finding him not guilty. Later, Rose's family brought a lawsuit against the city of Pittsburgh alleging that the city's police department was responsible for Rose's wrongful death. The city settled out of court with the Rose family, agreeing to pay them $2 million.

Efforts to obtain justice in cases of police shootings have been mixed. In some cases, police officers have been acquitted of wrongdoing. In other cases, officers have been convicted and sentenced to prison. Financial settlements and prison terms send a strong message but no amount of money or jail time can bring back those who have been wrongfully killed by police.

# CHAPTER THREE

# Retail Racism

On an April morning in 2018, Rashon Nelson and Donte Robinson, two twenty-three-year-old African American men from Philadelphia, walked into a Starbucks in the city's tony Rittenhouse Square neighborhood and took their seats at a table. They had an appointment that morning with a local entrepreneur, Andrew Yaffe, to talk about buying a property as a business investment. In fact, they had met with Yaffe several times over a period of months and believed they were very close to sealing the deal with the white business-man that morning. "We were there for a real reason, a real deal that we were working on," Robinson said. "We put in a lot of time, energy, effort. . . . We were at a moment that could have a positive impact on a whole ladder of people, lives, families."[21]

A Starbucks employee approached Nelson and Robin-son and asked them if they wished to place an order. No, the two men said, not at this time. They asked, though, if they could use the coffee shop's restroom.

A few minutes later three Philadelphia police officers en-tered the coffee shop. They approached Nelson and Rob-inson and ordered them to leave the premises. Nelson and Robinson refused. They were immediately placed in hand-cuffs and led out of the coffee shop. As they were being hus-tled out of the Starbucks, Yaffe showed up and demanded to know what was going on. He was ignored. As for Nelson and Robinson, they kept silent—both men feared that if they

Rashon Nelson (left) and Donte Robinson (right) were arrested at a Starbucks in Philadelphia after a suspicious employee called the police. The two entrepreneurs were at the coffee shop to meet with a prospective investor.

protested too vigorously they would be physically abused by the arresting officers. "When you know that you did nothing wrong, how do you really react to it?" Nelson said later. "You can either be ignorant or you can show some type of sophistication and act like you have class. That was the choice we had."[22]

Nelson and Robinson were taken to a city jail and placed in a cell. Finally, late that evening, they were released. The Philadelphia district attorney's office found no reason to charge the two men with criminal conduct and directed the police department to let them go.

## Stereotyped as Shoplifters

The arrests of Nelson and Robinson illustrate a level of bias against black people that many African Americans find to be all too common: when they walk into stores, restaurants, and other places of business, white employees are often suspicious of them. They often believe the black patrons may be there with the sole purpose of committing crimes. Many white store clerks suspect that the black customers may be shoplifters, or perhaps that they are concealing guns and plan to commit armed robbery. Sociologists call this trend "retail racism." "Name a store, any store, from Fifth Avenue to Main Street, and I'll bet that I can find a black person who has experienced discrimination there," says Cassi Pittman Claytor, a professor of sociology at Case Western Reserve University in Cleveland, Ohio. "Experiences of 'shopping while black' include everything from slights, like being ignored in favor of a white patron, to serious attacks on dignity and liberty, like being detained and questioned after making a purchase or handcuffed on suspicion of shoplifting."[23]

In fact, black people do not fit the profile of the typical shoplifter because there is no profile of typical shoplifters. According to the National Association for Shoplifting Prevention, an organization that advises merchants on how to prevent shoplifting in their stores, the typical shoplifter is neither black nor white, old nor young, male nor female. "Can you picture the typical shoplifter? If you can't, it's for good reason, because experts cite that there is no average shoplifter profile,"[24] says Stacy Weckesser, a writer who reports on consumer issues.

> "Name a store, any store, from Fifth Avenue to Main Street, and I'll bet that I can find a black person who has experienced discrimination there."[23]
>
> —Cassi Pittman Claytor, sociologist

Moreover, the stereotype of the typical shoplifter—a young black man from a poor urban neighborhood—couldn't be further from the truth. A study by Columbia University in New York City found that shoplifting is more likely to be committed by perpetrators who have higher incomes and educations. This suggests that most shoplifters do not commit their crimes for economic gain, but because of mental health issues that prompt those perpetrators to steal.

Still, there is no question that black shoppers are often suspected of shoplifting. That's what happened in 2018 to Dirone Taylor, Mekhi Lee, and Eric Rogers II, three African American

The stereotype of a poor urban black youth as the typical shoplifter is unfounded, according to a study done by Columbia University in New York City. Shoplifting is more likely to be committed by perpetrators who have higher incomes and educations.

teenagers who were shopping at a Nordstrom Rack clothing store in the St. Louis, Missouri, suburb of Brentwood. While the three young people were browsing among the racks of clothes in the stores—looking for clothes to wear to their high school prom—police officers showed up in the store and questioned the teens. The officers had been summoned by store employees. Soon, police determined the teenagers were not shoplifters and departed. "I felt like I was unequal," Rogers said. "By them calling the police, with everything going on, anything we could have done could have affected us, and could have drastically affected our lives. In a way, I was scared. But I couldn't show it."[25]

# Racial Profiling

Taylor, Lee, and Rogers were victims of an attitude by many white people and others known as racial profiling. In other words, the three young people were profiled as troublemakers for no reason other than that they are black. This stereotype continues to exist in the retail world, haunting African Americans such as the three innocent teenagers in the St. Louis suburb. But even African American celebrities report cases of racial profiling and retail racism. In 2015, John Henson, then a player for the Milwaukee Bucks in the National Basketball Association, attempted to enter a jewelry store in the Wisconsin community of Whitefish Bay. Henson had played for the Bucks since 2012—his photograph constantly appeared in the sports pages of Wisconsin newspapers, and Bucks games were televised throughout the state. Arriving at the store, Henson intended to buy a Rolex, a very expensive wristwatch. (A Rolex may cost as little as $5,000 and as much as $75,000.) According to Henson, as he approached the store a white employee rushed to lock the front door. Henson rang the doorbell twice, but the employees inside refused to unlock the door, even though he had arrived during regular business hours. What he didn't know was that the store employees had called police.

When police officers arrived they questioned Henson about his intentions and even asked him about the expensive car he was driving, indicating that they suspected him of stealing the vehicle. After learning that Henson was a highly paid professional basketball player, the police backed off. "This was one of the most degrading and racially prejudiced things I've ever experienced in life and wouldn't wish this on anyone,"[26] Henson said after the incident.

> "This was one of the most degrading and racially prejudiced things I've ever experienced in life and wouldn't wish this on anyone."[26]
>
> —John Henson, NBA star

The fact that Henson as well as Nelson, Robinson, and the three Brentwood teens were subjected to retail racism shows how deeply the problem is ingrained in society. Moreover, the incidents

# Racism and Facial Recognition

In recent years, cell phone manufacturers have introduced facial recognition software into their phones. In other words, a user no longer has to type in a code to unlock the phone. In a phone equipped with facial recognition software, all the user needs to do is hold the phone up to his or her face. At that point, the phone recognizes its owner and unlocks, enabling the owner to use the device.

But in 2017, shortly after rolling out early versions of their facial recognition features, phone manufacturers started receiving complaints—mostly from African American owners. It seems the facial recognition software was often unable to recognize black faces. The problem, according to software engineers, centered on the programming of the phones' software. The software had to be trained to recognize black faces. Simply put, the engineers who designed the programming for the phones did not expose the software to enough black faces during its developmental phase.

Members of Congress investigating the use of facial recognition software contend that very subtle racial biases are programmed into the software. According to US senator Ron Wyden of Oregon, white engineers give little thought to African American users when they programmed the facial recognition feature into the software. He said, "Any company or government that deploys new technology has a responsibility to scrutinize their product for bias and discrimination at least as thoroughly as they'd look for bugs in the software."

Quoted in Drew Harwell, "Federal Study Confirms Racial Bias of Many Facial-Recognition Systems, Casts Doubt on Their Expanding Use," *Washington Post*, December 19, 2019. www.washingtonpost.com.

illustrate that retail racism can occur anywhere. Whitefish Bay is a suburban community in Wisconsin; 85 percent of the citizens are white and less than 3 percent are African American. The white population of Brentwood is similar—in the St. Louis suburb, 87 percent of the population is white, while African Americans compose less than 3 percent of the population. Philadelphia, on the other hand, is a diverse big city in which 44 percent of the citizens are African American.

Moreover, the fact that the incident in Philadelphia occurred at a Starbucks came as a shock to executives of the company, who thought they had made diversity and equality a pillar of the company's culture. Indeed, prior to the incident in Philadelphia, Starbucks initiated a program to open its trendy coffee shops in numerous black communities—including Ferguson, Missouri, scene of the 2014 police shooting of Michael Brown. Moreover, the company has paid very close attention to its system of compensation and believed that it had attained 100 percent equality—that all employees, including women and minorities— were paid equally. And so, even though the incident occurred at a store owned by a company that prided itself on its accomplishments in achieving diversity, the arrests of Nelson and Robinson still showed that retail racism is very much a part of the fabric of American culture.

## Insulting the Secretary of State

Retail racism owes its existence to the same reasons that bias exists elsewhere in America: many white people distrust and fear black people—prejudices that have become ingrained in American society over the course of the past four hundred years. "Research has consistently documented that African Americans encounter discriminatory treatment while shopping, and that retail workers, particularly in stores located in predominantly white neighborhoods, frequently display racial prejudice against black customers,"[27] says Pittman Claytor.

Frequently, Pittman Claytor says, black consumers face longer wait times for service in stores and restaurants. Or, while a black person is browsing among the racks in a store, he or she may find a security guard summoned by employees to stand nearby. Or, as the case involving Nelson and Robinson illustrates, they may be asked to leave the premises, and, if they refuse, police are summoned and take them into custody.

In 2018, the national polling firm Gallup Organization asked African Americans if they had experienced racial bias while shopping.

Two-thirds of the respondents said they had been subjected to racial prejudice in retail establishments.

Among the African Americans who have said they have experienced retail racism is Condoleezza Rice, who served as secretary of state under President George W. Bush. The secretary of state is the nation's top diplomat—he or she is responsible for negotiating treaties, easing international tensions, and maintaining close relations with America's foreign allies.

Before she ascended to the position, Rice earned a PhD in international studies and served in numerous diplomatic roles for the US State Department. She also served on the faculty of Stanford University in California. These jobs typically included high salaries. Nevertheless, Rice recalled that while shopping in a department store near the Stanford campus in Palo Alto, California, she asked a white sales clerk to see some earrings. The clerk showed Rice some inexpensive samples of costume jewelry. Rice suspected that the white clerk didn't think she could afford the more expensive earrings. Rice says she responded quite angrily to the clerk: "Let's get one thing straight. You're behind the counter because you have to work for $6 an hour. I'm on this side asking to see the good jewelry because I make considerably more. And I'm asking to see the good jewelry."[28] The clerk quickly showed the future secretary of state a more pricey selection of earrings.

## Higher Prices for Cars

Rice suspected the white sales clerk believed she could not afford the more expensive earrings. But that is just one form of racism found in the retail world. A study published in the professional journal *American Economic Review* focused on car sales. It found that car dealers in America routinely try to charge blacks higher prices for cars than they expect to receive from whites.

Unlike jewelry and other products—which are typically sold at prices set by the manufacturer as well as the retailers—most new and used cars have no real set prices. Each car may have a sticker price—the price that appears on a window sticker on the car as it sits on the dealer's lot—but

> "You're behind the counter because you have to work for $6 an hour. I'm on this side asking to see the good jewelry because I make considerably more."[28]
>
> —Condoleezza Rice, former US secretary of state

in car sales there is typically a lot of negotiation between the buyer and seller before the two sides arrive at a final price. Therefore, the final price for the car is rarely the price a buyer sees on the sticker.

The *American Economic Review* study found, though, that from the outset of the negotiations, black car buyers are initially asked to pay more. In Rice's case, the future secretary of state believed the store clerk didn't think she could afford the more expensive jewelry. But that thinking does not apply in car sales—after all, if the white car dealers would not expect the black customers to be able to afford the higher prices, why would they seek to charge them more?

The answer, according to the authors of the study, is because the white car dealers do not believe black customers are as shrewd as white customers. To test that assumption, the study drafted white and black customers to walk into car dealerships and begin negotiations with white automotive salespeople. In most cases, the study found, the black customers were initially asked to pay more. Moreover, the study found, when the negotiations between the buyers and dealers ended, the final prices for the black buyers were typically higher than the prices paid by white buyers. "This is weird," noted journalist Derek Thompson.

> Black families have lower average household income than white families. Why would dealers ask them to pay higher prices? Okay, maybe they're just bigots. But maybe dealers aren't making a judgment about their customers' ability to pay; they're making a judgment about their customers' knowledge. . . . It's possible that these dealers expected white men to be smarter about cars. So they offered a better price. It's possible dealers thought blacks could be duped. So they offered a higher price. In fact, even in the haggling process, white men managed to eke out a better deal on the car."[29]

## Taking Their Business Elsewhere

Black people say they generally do know when they are being duped. Rice knew the sales clerk didn't think she could pay for the more expensive jewelry. In Rice's case, she demanded to see the more expensive earrings. Other black people respond differently: they walk out of the store. "When shopping while black happens to me, I take my business elsewhere," says Michelle Singletary, a personal finance columnist for the *Washington Post*. "And I hope the time will come when the color of my skin doesn't result in retail racism."[30]

> "When shopping while black happens to me, I take my business elsewhere."[30]
>
> —Michelle Singletary, personal finance columnist for the *Washington Post*

## Bias in the Corporate Suite

One of the reasons black shoppers may face bias in restaurants and stores is that the employees of those businesses are not instructed to treat everyone fairly. And one of the reasons those employees lack that instruction is that the major corporations that operate those retail establishments often lack African American executives who would ensure that employees treat all customers equally.

According to a 2019 report by the National Opinion Research Center at the University of Chicago, just four of the chief executive officers (CEOs) at the five hundred largest corporations in America are black. Moreover, just 3.8 percent of senior management employees at those corporations are black. "With blacks making up 10 percent of college graduates, you would think there would be 50 black CEOs. But there are only four," said Pooja Jain-Link, who worked on the study.

Jain-Link said black employees often face racial bias as they try to climb up corporate ladders. The study queried nearly four thousand respondents who work in corporate executive offices, including 520 black employees. According to the study, 65 percent of the black employees said racial bias is a factor in their inability to advance into their corporations' top jobs. Said Joseph B. Hill, an African American executive in the health care field, "It's troubling that no matter how much or how loudly professional blacks share that their experience is challenging simply because of their race it is often not believed or valued by their white counterparts. And that's where much of the problems lie."

Quoted in Curtis Bunn, "Blacks in Corporate America Still Largely Invisible, Study Finds," NBC News, December 11, 2019. www.nbcnews.com.

Despite Singletary's optimism that in the future retail racism will cease haunting black customers as they shop for jewelry, expensive watches, clothes, and cars, it would seem that for now many black people can expect the same type of treatment they have always faced. They can expect to encounter suspicious store clerks who are quick to call the police whenever African American shoppers walk into their stores.

# CHAPTER FOUR

# Bias on Campus

Andrew Johnson's coach and teammates at Buena Regional High School in New Jersey regarded the 120-pound wrestler as one of the team's toughest competitors. During his sophomore year on the team, he finished with a record of 13–12. He vowed to do better in his junior year. In December 2018, Johnson stepped onto the mat to face an opponent from nearby Oakcrest High School.

There was a lot riding on the match. Buena Regional and Oakcrest were regarded as the two top teams in the National Division of New Jersey's Cape Atlantic League, with the winner of the meet expected to go on to the division title. But as Johnson approached his opponent to begin the match, the referee, Alan Maloney, stepped between the two wrestlers. Maloney told Johnson that his hairstyle violated league rules and that he could not compete unless he cut his hair.

Johnson, whose father is black and mother is Hispanic, had let his hair grow into dreadlocks—a hairstyle that features rope-like clumps of long matted hair. According to Maloney, the rules of the New Jersey State Interscholastic Athletic Association, the governing body overseeing high school sports in the state, prohibited a wrestler's hair from falling below the competitor's shirt collar, earlobes or eyebrows. Maloney told Johnson he would have to cut off his dreadlocks or forfeit the match. He gave the wrestler ninety seconds to decide.

Johnson was clearly distraught by the referee's order. But he turned to his team's trainer and told her to cut off his dreadlocks. The trainer gave Johnson a quick and sloppy cut that, nevertheless, met the league rules. As the trainer snipped through his dreadlocks, cries of "Noooo!" could be heard raining down from the gymnasium stands.

At first, it appeared the trauma of the incident had affected Johnson as he quickly fell behind on points to his opponent. But he rallied, forced the match into overtime and emerged with the victory. Johnson's win helped Buena Regional defeat Oakcrest that day and, later, win the National Division title. As for Johnson, minutes after the match against Oakcrest his mother found him in the hallway outside the gymnasium. He was weeping.

*Andrew Johnson, pictured on the left, is a high school wrestler from New Jersey. A white referee told Johnson he would have to cut off his dreadlocks or forfeit a match. Johnson had his team's trainer cut off his dreadlocks. Johnson was the target of bias—a decision by a white referee to enforce an old-time rule that had been ignored virtually everywhere else in New Jersey high school athletics.*

## Foreign and Unacceptable

Johnson had just experienced a form of bias—a decision by a white referee to enforce an old-time rule that evidently had been ignored virtually everywhere else in New Jersey high school athletics. Indeed, a video of the match was posted on social media, and observers couldn't help but notice that Johnson's white opponent, Dave Flippen, also wore his hair in a length and style that may have been in violation of the rules. "Watching the video, there are moments where Flippen's hair flops past his eyebrows, which is supposed to be illegal,"[31] says journalist Jesse Washington.

In this case, the bias leveled against Johnson took the form of a very subtle reminder that some white people find African American culture both foreign and unacceptable. "Today, dreadlocks have been adopted by men and women all over the world, but have been most closely associated with black culture," says Milton W. Hinton Jr., a civil rights leader in New Jersey.

> "Dreadlocks are intimidating to many people. Dreadlocks scare them to death and make them very uncomfortable. . . . So, fear prompts many to react unreasonably to this strange, 'foreign' hairstyle. I have both male and female friends who have worn 'locs' for decades and say that when they go out in public, others on the sidewalk stop, stare and let them pass as if Moses were once again parting the Red Sea. It would be funny if it were not so sad."[32]

"Dreadlocks are intimidating to many people. Dreadlocks scare them to death and make them very uncomfortable."[32]

—Milton W. Hinton Jr., New Jersey civil rights leader

In this case, the bias against African Americans surfaced on the grounds of an American high school—a place where students learn about US history and culture and how diversity is supposed to be a fundamental goal of American society. Bias against black people still exists on high school and college campuses as well. Sometimes

## Suicide Rates Among Black Students

A 2019 study by the American Academy of Pediatrics reported that suicide rates for African American young people between the ages of twelve and eighteen increased by 73 percent between 1991 and 2017. In contrast, the study found that suicide rates for white young people fell by 7.5 percent during the same time. The study analyzed some two hundred thousand cases of suicide or attempted suicide by youths during that time frame.

The coauthor of the study, Sean Joe, a sociologist at Washington University in St. Louis, Missouri, said young black people are often exposed to racial bias, which can have an effect on their mental health and the reason they harbor notions of suicide. He said, "The rise in suicide rates among black youth can most likely be traced back to an internalization of issues around structural racism in America."

Joe also pointed out that a reason for the increasing suicide rate among African American youths may be due to the fact that black students may not have access to mental health counseling often available to white students. Many schools attended by African American students are in poor urban neighborhoods. Such schools often lack funding that would provide mental health counseling to troubled black students. Said Joe, "[There is] a lack of investment in mental health services in black communities."

Quoted in Neil Schoenherr, "Suicide Attempts Among Black Adolescents on the Rise," Washington University in St. Louis, October 22, 2019. https://source.wustl.edu.

the bias can be subtle—such as when a white referee orders an African American student to shed a harmless and popular hairstyle. But other times, the bias is far from subtle: Black students on high school and college campuses have encountered vehement and ugly racism. And, very often, they have found that their fellow students—the people who sit across the aisle from them in their classrooms—are at the center of this racist behavior.

## Taking Racist Attitudes to School

In September 2019, overt racism greeted black students from Lincoln High School in San Diego, California, when they traveled to nearby San Clemente High School for a football game. During the game, Lincoln High football players and cheerleaders heard racial slurs and taunts from San Clemente students and adults who attended the game. Some of the cheerleaders said they were harassed while they were trying to buy refreshments or use the restrooms.

The racial slurs became so blatant that faculty members accompanying the cheerleaders to San Clemente High School escorted the young women out of the stadium and to their bus before the game ended. "During the game, multiple spectators heckled the Lincoln players and cheer squad, repeatedly using racial slurs," said Clovis Honoré, president of the San Diego branch of the NAACP, a civil rights organization. "Furthermore, cheer squad members were racially harassed in restrooms. . . . This harassment came not only from high-school-age youth but also from adult fans."[33]

> "During the game, multiple spectators heckled the Lincoln players and cheer squad, repeatedly using racial slurs."[33]
>
> —Clovis Honoré, president of the San Diego branch of the NAACP

As with the case of the bias faced by Johnson, the bias at San Clemente High School surfaced on the campus of an educational institution. Noel Jacob Kent, a professor of ethnic studies at the University of Hawaii, examined the issue of racism on campuses and drew the conclusion that students often reflect the values they learn at home. Therefore, Kent found, if a student is exposed to racist attitudes expressed by parents or others at home, the student will likely take those attitudes to school. "Why so much bigotry and intolerance at institutions long seen as dedicated to reason and the search for truth?" asked Kent. "Part of the answer is that life on campus closely mirrors the dominant patterns and attitudes of the larger society. In both, racial structures and meanings are in flux and hotly contested and racism, driven by a profound 'moral crisis,' has proven an entrenched and virulent social force."[34]

## In Times of Economic Stress

Kent also found that racist incidents often surface during times of economic stress. He said that when people are out of work or otherwise find themselves financially strapped, they often seek others to blame for their misfortunes. And, very often, they choose to blame minority groups. He says, "Our economy . . . is going through its most profound restructuring—diminished opportunity, stagnating wages, a decline in the quality of life for many families directly conflict with the mythic American dream. The result: depression, confusion, and wide-ranging anger throughout the society, a reaction that the campus is not immune from."[35]

High schools are not the only places of learning that experience racism. Racism can also be found at colleges and universities. This reality confounds sociologists, civil rights leaders, and others who study bias. After all, college campuses have largely been the

Colleges have largely been places where people of all races and faiths come together to study and learn from each other. Yet racism still persists on campuses across the country.

foundations of American progressivism—places where people of all races and faiths come together to study and learn from each other. In fact, back in the 1960s college students were among the first Americans to demonstrate for equality and an end to segregation. In the summer of 1965, many white college students in the northern states boarded buses and headed to the South to participate in a drive known as the SCOPE Project (SCOPE stands for Summer Community Organization and Political Education). The purpose of the drive was to assist black citizens to register to vote in communities where white politicians were devising strategies to deny African Americans their right to cast ballots.

Bruce Miroff was a college student in 1965 when he volunteered to help register black citizens in James Island, South Carolina. He recalls,

> When we first came to James Island and were going door-to-door, I remember a small child saying, "Mom, it's the insurance man," because the only white people they ever saw were insurance men collecting premiums. By the last week we were working—we were so familiar to the community that a child answered the door and yelled back to his mother, "Mom, it's the voting man."[36]

## Lynching Display on Campus

While that type of passion for inclusion and diversity may still be found on many college campuses more than fifty years later, racial bias is also widely found on college campuses today. Jailyn Gladney, an African American former student at Boston University in Massachusetts, says she attended freshman orientation at her school in the summer of 2012. Gladney says she and the other students were told about the liberal atmosphere on campus—how all students should feel accepted. "At orientation, the deans and the police told us a lot of things about how to stay safe both on and off campus. They fed us visions of a liberal

## School Suspension Rates

Black students in public schools are nearly four times more likely than white students to be suspended, according to a 2018 report by the US Department of Education. The report found that 5 percent of white students are typically suspended for disciplinary measures. In contrast, nearly 18 percent of black students are suspended.

Minnesota had one of the highest levels of suspension among black students. According to the Education Department, black students in Minnesota are eight times more likely to be suspended than white students.

Bernadeia Johnson, an African American and former superintendent of schools in Minneapolis, Minnesota, believes racial bias by teachers is at the heart of the stricter discipline measures leveled at African American students. As superintendent, Johnson looked into suspensions in the Minneapolis schools and found notes written by teachers regarding students who had been disciplined. Typical of the notes, she said, are descriptions of white children by teachers who spoke of the students as "gifted but can't use his words" and "high strung," with their actions excused because they "had a hard day." As for black students, the notes typically described them as "destructive," "violent," and "cannot be managed." Said Johnson, "When you see something like that and you're a leader, and you're trying to figure out how to move the school system forward—it was alarming."

Quoted in Erica L. Green, "Why Are Black Students Punished So Often? Minnesota Confronts a National Quandary," *New York Times*, March 18, 2018. www.nytimes.com.

university with 'good' white people who believed in progressive and diverse education and perspectives,"[37] she says.

And yet soon after classes started, Gladney's African American boyfriend, also a student at Boston University, was stopped and questioned by city police as he walked along a street a few blocks off campus. Police told him they suspected him of looking

> "They fed us visions of a liberal university with 'good' white people who believed in progressive and diverse education and perspectives."[37]
>
> —Jailyn Gladney, former Boston University student

over parked cars with the intention of stealing a vehicle. She also related another incident in which a drunken white student attending a campus party started uttering racial slurs toward black students. And Gladney recalled seeing posters plastered across campus stating "I support Dylann Roof." Roof is the white supremacist who walked into a black church in Charleston, South Carolina, in 2015 and opened fire, killing nine African American churchgoers. "For black students, every day on campus is a reminder that we aren't welcome,"[38] says Gladney.

As Gladney says, her campus experiences were not unusual. In 2020, students who walked into a campus gift shop at Michigan State University were shocked to see a display of black dolls hanging from a toy tree—as though they had been lynched in the Jim Crow South. The dolls resembled famous figures, among them former president Barack Obama and Prince, the black pop star who died from an opioid drug overdose in 2016. Altogether, about a half-dozen similar trees were displayed in the shop. Krystal Rose Davis-Dunn, an African American student at Michigan State who saw the displays, said, "It's African-American people hanging from twine. That is problematic. You're lynching black people from trees."[39] Ironically, the gift shop that featured the racist displays is located in a building named in honor of Clifton R. Wharton, an African American and former president of the university.

At Syracuse University in New York State, several examples of racist graffiti showed up on the walls of a freshman dormitory in November 2019. The school administration responded by trying to keep the graffiti incident quiet. The walls were quickly scrubbed clean while university officials met with residents of the dormitory to assure them steps were being taken to ensure their safety.

And yet, as university maintenance workers scrubbed the racist graffiti off the dormitory wall, other examples of racist graffiti were discovered on campus. One African American student told a reporter, "For a lot of students, this place is heaven. But for students of color, it's been hell."[40]

## Rise of the Alt-Right

Some experts argue that incidents like these are being fueled by the Alt-Right movement, which has established chapters at many universities in order to spread its racist rhetoric among young people. Short for "Alternative Right," the movement grew during the decade of the 2010s, drawing racist whites to demonstrations across the country. Alt-Right activists also maintain a strong presence on the internet as well as social media. The activists denounce immigration into the United States and have expressed hateful rhetoric targeting African Americans, Hispanics, Jews, Muslims, and gays.

The Anti-Defamation League (ADL), which monitors bias against Jews in America, issued a report in 2019 chronicling the rise of Alt-Right activity on college campuses. The report noted that the movement had been active on 122 college campuses in thirty-three different states during the 2018–2019

*Alt-Right protesters wave flags at a rally in Portland, Oregon, in 2019. Some experts argue that racism on campus is being fueled by the Alt-Right movement, which has established chapters at many universities to spread its racist rhetoric.*

academic year. Typically, the ADL found, Alt-Right activists fanned out on campuses, handing out literature or posting placards expressing their racist beliefs.

Citing the ADL report, the publication *Inside Higher Ed* stated,

> They have been increasingly targeting colleges and universities since January 2016, and began appearing in larger numbers in the fall semester of that year. . . . More than three years later their materials—fliers, stickers, posters—continue to proliferate on campuses. The posters often contain insignias and other white nationalist images and are used to direct students and others to social media. White supremacists often target campuses because they want to recruit young extremists to their ranks.[41]

"White supremacists often target campuses because they want to recruit young extremists to their ranks."[41]

—*Inside Higher Ed* magazine

Incidents of bias are often the acts of individuals such as the referee who made Andrew Johnson cut off his dreadlocks or the drunken student encountered at a campus party by Jailyn Gladney. Many racially biased incidents are committed as part of an organized effort planned by Alt-Right groups. And so, there is no question that racial bias has found a place at American high schools and colleges. Long considered to be centers of progressive ideals, diversity, and inclusion, high school and college campuses are clearly not immune to bias against African Americans and members of other minority groups.

# CHAPTER FIVE

# Confronting Bias

Minutes after Michael Brown was killed by Ferguson police officer Darren Wilson, neighbors poured out of their houses and gathered around his body. Ferguson's detectives and medical examiners dispatched to investigate the shooting were slow to respond to the scene. In fact, Brown's body was not taken out of the street until four hours after the shooting. In the meantime, dozens of neighbors gathered around the body, watching in disgust as blood seeped out of the dead man's wounds. "The delay helped fuel the outrage," said Patricia Bynes, an African American political leader in Ferguson. "It was very disrespectful to the community and the people who live there. It also sent the message from law enforcement that 'we can do this to you any day, any time, in broad daylight, and there's nothing you can do about it.'"[42]

Over the coming days, the anger and grief felt by the black citizens of Ferguson continued to grow. Neighbors set up a small memorial at the scene of the shooting, placing flowers, photos of Brown, and stuffed animals on the street—but a police car ran over the memorial, crushing and scattering the objects meant to honor the life of Brown. Many of the residents saw this act as a callous disregard for the Ferguson residents mourning the death of the young man. The next day, hundreds of angry citizens of Ferguson began demonstrating on the streets of the community. They

Neighbors set up a small memorial near where black teenager Michael Brown was shot to death by a white police officer in 2014. Later a police car ran over the memorial, crushing the objects meant to honor the life of Brown.

marched, chanted, and sang, refusing to disperse when ordered to do so by police. Many of the marchers shouted the words, "Hands up, don't shoot!"—a reference to the reports that Brown had raised his hands to surrender to Wilson but was shot anyway.

In fact, in what became known as the Ferguson Uprising, protests, rioting, and looting continued in the Missouri city for eleven days. Riot police had to be called in to dispel angry crowds. Sporadic violence continued to break out for months after the shooting. Says Barbara Ransby, a professor of African American studies at the University of Chicago,

By all indications, Michael Brown was not a saint. However, in the resistance that followed his death, organizers insisted he did not have to be. There did not have to be a correlation between "sainthood" and black citizenship. This was an important shift in the discourse about who is or is not a sympathetic victim of injustice. Brown did not have to be a church-going, law-abiding, proper-speaking embodiment of respectability in order for his life to matter, protesters insisted. And they insisted loudly.[43]

## Black Lives Matter

Ransby's insistence that Brown's life mattered was echoed by many protesters not only in Ferguson but across the country as well. In the weeks following the Ferguson shooting, a movement that became known as Black Lives Matter emerged.

The movement had its roots in other protests that had been staged in the two years before the Brown shooting. In 2012, Trayvon Martin, a seventeen-year-old African American, was shot and killed by George Zimmerman, a member of his Florida gated community's volunteer town watch team. A group known as a Million Hoodies for Justice soon came together and organized protests over the shooting of the teenager. Later that year, a second group, the Dream Defenders, staged a protest march across Florida to demand justice for Martin. Zimmerman was eventually charged with killing Martin, but he was acquitted by a jury. In the aftermath of the Zimmerman trial, black activists started using the hashtag #blacklivesmatter to spread their message across social media.

It was the shooting of Brown, however, that prompted activists to take the campaign they had started on social media into the streets. Brown's death transformed the movement and the lives of those who have taken part in it. "If Mike wasn't killed and people weren't directly impacted, if we didn't leave our homes, I don't know where or what movement I would (have been in) two years ago,"[44] said Johnetta Elzie, twenty-seven, a Ferguson protester who has become a prominent voice in the Black Lives Matter movement.

Today, Black Lives Matter maintains chapters in fifteen American cities. In the years following the death of Brown, Black

Lives Matter has staged a number of protests—particularly after police shootings of African American citizens. In 2016, the group staged public protests outside the arenas hosting the Republican and Democratic national conventions, which were meeting to select their parties' nominees for president. And the organization has established the Black to the Future Action Fund, which it employs to raise campaign money for candidates who share the group's mission to end the victimization of black citizens by police.

One program pushed by the movement has been to convince police departments to equip officers with body cameras. The device is usually worn on the chest of the officer and is capable of capturing audio and video of the officer's confrontation with a suspect. If Wilson had been wearing a body camera, there would have been no question about whether Brown had charged him, as the police officer asserted, or whether Brown turned and raised his hands—as

*Supporters of the Black Lives Matter movement walk in Washington, DC, in 2014. The shooting of Michael Brown propelled the movement into a nationwide cause. Today, Black Lives Matter maintains chapters in fifteen American cities.*

witnesses reported. Many police departments have responded and are now routinely equipping police officers with body cameras. Says technology writer Ben Miller, "The technology was not new. But the events that unfolded in Ferguson took what used to be a relatively rare piece of hardware and turned it into . . . one of the most important trends in law enforcement and surveillance technology today."[45]

## Recruiting More Black Police Officers

In addition to equipping police officers with body cameras, many communities are stepping up their efforts to recruit black police officers. Many experts believe that incidents of police bias against black citizens would decrease if more of the officers responding to the scene are African American. Says, Patrick Oliver, an African American and the retired police chief of Cleveland, Ohio, "While African Americans report perceptions of police bias, even leading to a pervasive fear of police brutality, officer diversity can create confidence in a law enforcement agency's understanding of local issues and a perception of more positive interactions between officers and minorities."[46]

Following the fatal shooting of seventeen-year-old Antwon Rose II, the city of Pittsburgh stepped up its efforts to recruit black candidates for its police department. The city realized that just 13 percent of its police officers were black although African American citizens make up 25 percent of the city's population. Moreover, the city government issued a report finding that in 2018—the year Rose was shot—just four of the eighty-four students at the city's police academy were African American.

To find more candidates, officials from the city police department made a recruiting trip to Howard University, a historically black college in Washington, DC. The city also posted recruiting advertisements on social media platforms followed by African American students. And police department officials took part in career fairs held in the city's African American neighborhoods.

Dre Gordon responded to those recruitment efforts. A recent high school graduate from the nearby town of Emsworth, Pennsylvania, Gordon intends to apply to the Pittsburgh police academy. Gordon says that as an African American, he feels he can bring some sensitivity to the scene when he responds to calls in black neighborhoods. "That was one of the things that motivated me to say 'Yes, I want to be a police officer,'" he said. "Because I want to be in those situations because I feel like I could read those situations a little better."[47]

## Diversity Training

Efforts to reduce bias against black citizens have not been limited to police departments. Activist groups have come together and have been very vocal in protesting bias in other sectors of society as well, including incidents of retail racism. Social media has often played a role in spreading news about incidents of bias and providing formats for organizers to plan protests. For example,

the arrests of Rashon Nelson and Donte Robinson were recorded on cell phone video by customers in the Philadelphia Starbucks and soon posted on social media. Civil rights activists responded by staging protests in front of the Rittenhouse Square coffee shop as well as in front of other Starbucks stores across the nation. A few days after the arrests of Nelson and Robinson, dozens of protesters gathered outside the Rittenhouse Square Starbucks coffee shop. "We don't want this Starbucks to make any money today. That's our goal,"[48] said Abdul-Aliy Muhammad, one of the protest's organizers.

The activists called for a national boycott of Starbucks. Many customers participated in the boycott, refusing to stop in for their

**58**

# Backlash Against a Bookseller

Sometimes, well-intentioned efforts to promote diversity fall flat. That's what happened in 2020 when the Barnes & Noble chain of bookstores promoted the republication of numerous well-known books—but with black characters. Among the books featured in the "Diverse Editions" series were new editions of *The Wizard of Oz, Peter Pan, and Romeo and Juliet*—all featuring black characters on their covers.

The bookstore chain sought to stock its shelves with those books in an effort to engage black readers with the classic books, but black customers did not see it that way. They pointed out that the books do not tell stories of the black experience in America or other countries and instead merely substitute black characters for the white characters who were originally portrayed in the stories. Said Terri N. Watson, an African American and associate professor of educational leadership at City College of New York, "There are authors [of color] they could have highlighted, but they've simply put a new cover on an old book that's part of a canon, which is a problem because [the canon] lacks diversity."

After many complaints about the Diverse Editions books surfaced on social media, Barnes & Noble elected to cancel the series. In defending its attempt to sell the books, the company insisted that it had good intentions. "The booksellers who championed this initiative did so convinced it would help drive engagement with these classic titles," the company said in a statement.

Quoted in Valerie Reiss, "Recast Books Pulled as 'Literary Blackface,'" *Philadelphia Inquirer*, February 6, 2020, p. A3.

morning lattes and cappuccinos. Ultimately, the protests cost Starbucks nearly $17 million in sales. In response, one month after the arrest of Nelson and Robinson, Starbucks closed all its eight thousand stores for one day so that the company's 175,000 employees could receive training in recognizing the rights of people of all races. "The company's founding values are based on humanity and inclusion," said Howard Schultz, chairman of Starbucks. "We will learn from our mistakes and reaffirm

## America's Antilynching Law

More than a century after the measure was first proposed, the US House of Representatives in early 2020 passed a measure recognizing lynching as a federal crime. Over the years, a federal antilynching law failed to gain traction until US Representative Bobby Rush, an African American member of Congress from Illinois, introduced the measure in the House. The bill passed by a 410–4 vote and then moved to the Senate, where it awaited consideration.

A federal antilynching bill was first proposed in 1900, but efforts to adopt the legislation were blocked over the years by members of Congress from the South. Between 1882 and 1968, 4,743 people are believed to have died by lynching, most of them African Americans. Some 99 percent of the perpetrators are believed to have escaped punishment.

Although lynching has not been a common part of life in America for decades, Rush said he believes it is important to get the law on the books to send a message that the federal government believes the rights of all citizens should be recognized. "This act of American terrorism has to be repudiated," said Rush. "And now it's being repudiated. It's never too late to repudiate evil and this lynching is an American evil."

The measure is named the US Emmett Till Anti-Lynching Act. Till, fourteen, was beaten and lynched in the town of Money, Mississippi, by two white men in 1955. The perpetrators were eventually acquitted of his murder, although they later confessed to the crime.

Quoted in Claudia Grisales, "'It's About Time': House Approves Historic Bill Making Lynching a Federal Crime," National Public Radio, February 26, 2020, www.npr.org.

our commitment to creating a safe and welcoming environment for every customer."[49]

Other companies have also employed diversity training. In 2019, the cosmetics retailer Sephora found itself facing charges of retail racism when the pop star Solána Imani Rowe, known to her fans as SZA, charged on Twitter that a white employee of a Sephora store in Calabasas, California, summoned security guards to make sure she was not shoplifting. Sephora reacted quickly—the company closed all its stores for one hour so that all sixteen thousand employees could undergo diversity training. By closing their doors and requiring employees to go through diversity training, Starbucks and Sephora showed that they at least recognize they have bias problems among their employees and took steps toward ending retail racism in their stores.

## Addressing Racism on Campus

Many school administrators have responded similarly to reports of racial bias on campuses. At Syracuse University, where racist graffiti was painted on a dormitory wall in 2019, students staged protests demanding the university take action to prevent similar incidents in the future. The protests were organized on social media under the slogan #NotAgainSU. The protesters, including members of the black, Hispanic, Jewish, and Muslim communities, occupied the school's Schine Student Center, demanding the school take significant action to curb bias on campus. After nearly two weeks of the sit-in, school officials agreed to require diversity training for faculty members and other school employees and mandate classes in diversity for new students. Also, university officials agreed to upgrade security cameras on campus and double the number of patrols by campus security officers. Said Syracuse Chancellor Kent D. Syverud, "These last 10 days, I've talked to so many students and they're so afraid and angry. And I understand why."[50]

Racial bias on high school campuses is also being addressed. In New Jersey, the referee's order to Andrew Johnson, directing the high school wrestler to shed his dreadlocks, came under considerable scrutiny. After investigating the case, the New Jersey attorney general's office concluded that referee Alan Maloney's order to Johnson was racially biased. Maloney was ultimately suspended from officiating at high school wrestling meets for two years. In 2019, New Jersey governor Phil Murphy signed a state law prohibiting discrimination in schools or in the workplace based on the length or style of hair. "This law will ensure people of color are free to wear their hair however they feel best represents them, whether that be locks, braids, twists, or curls," said state senator Sandra B. Cunningham, who sponsored the legislation. "No one should ever be told it is 'unprofessional' to embrace their culture."[51] New York and California adopted similar measures; by 2020, another thirteen states were considering their own laws recognizing the rights of people to wear their hair as they choose.

As for Johnson, he resumed wrestling for his high school team for the 2019–2020 season—his senior year. Dominic Spezali, an attorney representing Johnson, said the young wrestler hopes to put the incident behind him and get on with his life and his passion for wrestling. "It's a lot to bear on his shoulders," Spezali said. "He should have never been put through this."[52]

## Recruiting More Black Teachers

Educators believe one way to confront racism on campus is to recruit more African Americans as teachers, much as many police departments have sought to recruit more black candidates to serve as police officers. According to the US Education Department, in 2016 there were about 3.8 million public school teachers in America. Even though 15 percent of public school students are black, the report noted, 80 percent of those teachers are white and 7 percent are black. Quan Neloms, a high school guidance counselor in Detroit, Michigan, says employing more black teachers can have a positive impact on black students. Neloms says many black students regard black teachers as role models. "Statistics show that particularly for a male student, when they encounter a teacher that looks like them, resembles them, they tend to have a better experience in school,"[53] says Neloms.

And a better experience in school may lead a young black student into college

"Statistics show that particularly for a male student, when they encounter a teacher that looks like them, resembles them, they tend to have a better experience in school."[53]

—Quan Neloms, high school guidance counselor

and eventually a well-paying career rather than into life on an urban street, where he or she may struggle to find meaningful employment. A 2018 study by Johns Hopkins University in Baltimore, Maryland, found that 13 percent of black students who had one black teacher were more likely to enroll in college. That number increased to 32 percent when students had two black teachers. "Having a positive black . . . role model, the students are less likely to drop out of school and more likely to finish high school, and more likely to be happy about coming to school every day," says Chris Rutherford, of the Campaign for Black Male Achievement, which helps young black male students complete their high school educations. "Part of this comes from just having that relationship, having someone near that provides a difference."[54]

In the four hundred years since black slaves first arrived on US shores, Americans have struggled with racial bias. For hundreds of years, charges of racism were largely ignored. But now, many individuals and institutions take the issue of racial bias very seriously. Many police departments, retailers, and schools are now quicker to respond to charges of racism than they once were. Although much remains to be done, many people are working to one day ensure the equality of all races in American society.

# SOURCE NOTES

## Introduction: Some Ugly Truths

1. Quoted in Kevin Krause, "Ex-Firefighter Who Hung Doll with Noose to Threaten Black Neighbors Gets Year in Prison for Hate Crime," *Dallas Morning News*, October 24, 2018. www.dallasnews.com.
2. Krause, "Ex-Firefighter."
3. Quoted in Ken Belson, "Only Three NFL Head Coaches Are Black. 'It's Embarrassing,'" *New York Times*, December 31, 2019. www.nytimes.com.
4. Quoted in Nick Shook, "Roger Goodell: We Need to Evaluate the Rooney Rule," NFL.com, January 29, 2020. www.nfl.com.

## Chapter One: Struggles Against Racism

5. Glenn C. Loury, "An American Tragedy: The Legacy of Slavery Lingers in Our Cities' Ghettos," Brookings Institution, March 1, 1998. www.brookings.edu.
6. Quoted in Walter E. Williams, "Setting the Record Straight on the '3/5 Compromise,'" Tenth Amendment Center, November 12, 2015. https://tenthamendment center.com.
7. Harriet Ann Jacobs, *Incidents in the Life of a Slave Girl*. Boston: L. Maria Child, 1891, pp. 25–27.
8. Quoted in William H. Chafe, Raymond Gavins, and Robert Korstad, eds., *Remembering Jim Crow: African Americans Tell About Life in the Segregated South*. New York: New Press, 2014, p. 8.
9. Quoted in Ralph Ginzburg, *100 Years of Lynching*. Baltimore: Black Classic Press, 1988, p. 15.
10. Quoted in Steven D. Farough, "Rebuilding or Reloading," in *American Identity in the Age of Obama,* Amílcar Antonio Barreto and Richard L. O'Bryant, eds. New York: Routledge, 2014, p. 152.

## Chapter Two: Victimized by Police

11. Jennifer Cobbina, *Hands Up, Don't Shoot: Why the Protests in Ferguson and Baltimore Matter, and How They Changed America*. New York: New York University Press, 2019, p. 5.

12. Quoted in Amina Kahn, "Getting Killed by Police Is a Leading Cause of Death for Young Black Men in America," *Los Angeles Times*, August 16, 2019. www.latimes.com.

13. Quoted in Kahn, "Getting Killed by Police."

14. Quoted in Cassandra Chaney and Ray V. Robertson, "Racism and Police Brutality in America," *Journal of African American Studies*, 2013, p. 483.

15. Chaney and Robertson, "Racism and Police Brutality," p. 483.

16. E. Ashby Plant and B. Michelle Peruche, "The Consequences of Race for Police Officers' Responses to Criminal Suspects," *Psychological Science*, March 2005, p. 182.

17. Plant and Peruche, "Consequences of Race," p. 180.

18. Quoted in Jake Halpern, "The Cop," *New Yorker*, August 3, 2015. www.newyorker.com.

19. US Justice Department, "Attorney General Holder Delivers Update on Investigations in Ferguson, Missouri," March 4, 2015. www.justice.gov.

20. Quoted in Colin Dwyer, "Former SC Officer Who Killed Walter Scott Sentenced to 20 Years in Prison," National Public Radio, December 7, 2017. www.npr.org.

## Chapter Three: Retail Racism

21. Quoted in *The Guardian* (Manchester, UK), "Black Men Arrested at Philadelphia Starbucks Feared for Their Lives," April 19, 2018. www.theguardian.com.

22. Quoted in *The Guardian*, "Black Men Arrested."

23. Cassi Pittman Claytor, "'Shopping While Black': Yes, Bias Against Black Customers Is Real," *The Guardian* (Manchester, UK), June 24, 2019. www.theguardian.com.

24. Stacy Weckesser, "The Five-Finger Discount: 35 Facts About Shoplifting in America," September 25, 2018. https://bluewatercredit.com.

25. Quoted in Aaron Smith and Marlena Baldacci, "Nordstrom Rack Apologizes for Falsely Accusing Black Teens of Stealing," CNN.com, May 8, 2018. https://money.cnn.com.

26. Lisa Gutierrez, "Shoppers Fighting Back Against 'Shopping While Black' Profiling with Social Media, Lawsuits," *Kansas City (MO) Star*, November 6, 2015. www.kansascity.com.

27. Cassie Pittman Claytor, "'Shopping While Black': Black Consumers' Management of Racial Stigma and Racial Profiling in Retail Settings," *Journal of Consumer Culture*, July 2017, p. 2.

28. Quoted in Juliet Lapidos, "The Condensed Condoleezza Rice," Slate.com, December 17, 2007. https://slate.com.

29. Derek Thompson, "The Price Is Racist: When Minorities (and Women) Are Asked to Pay More," *The Atlantic*, June 24, 2013. www.theatlantic.com.

30. Michelle Singletary, "Shopping While Black. African Americans Continue to Face Retail Racism," *Washington Post*, May 17, 2018. www.washingtonpost.com.

## Chapter Four: Bias on Campus

31. Jesse Washington, "The Untold Story of Wrestler Andrew Johnson's Dreadlocks," TheUndefeated.com, September 18, 2019. https://theundefeated.com.

32. Milton W. Hinton Jr., "Dread of Dreadlocks Stokes Unfairness for Wrestler," NJ.com, January 29, 2019. www.nj.com.

33. Quoted in Malik Earnest, "Lincoln High Cheerleaders Taunted with Racial Slurs," Fox 5, September 16, 2019. https://fox5sandiego.com.

34. Noel Jacob Kent, "The New Campus Racism: What's Going On?" *NEA High Education Journal*, Fall 2000, p. 83.

35. Kent, "The New Campus Racism," pp. 83–84.

36. Quoted in Nick Miroff, "Veterans of '60s Voter-Registration Drive Reflect," National Public Radio, August 6, 2005. www.npr.org.

37. Jailyn Gladney, "Boston University Is Proof That University Campuses Are Anything but 'Post-racial,'" *The Nation*, July 14, 2015. www.thenation.com.

38. Gladney, "Boston University."

39. Quoted in Mark Johnson, "Michigan College Gift Shop Removes Doll Display Depicting Black Leaders Hanging from Tree," *Providence (RI) Journal*, February 4, 2020, www.providencejournal.com.
40. Quoted in Aaron Randle, "Racial Slurs, and the 15 Days That Shook Syracuse," *New York Times*, November 17, 2019. www.nytimes.com.
41. Jeremy Bauer-Wolf , "White Supremacy Activity Spreads on Campuses," *Inside Higher Ed*, June 27, 2019. www.insidehighered.com.

## Chapter Five: Confronting Bias

42. Quoted in Julie Bosman and Joseph Goldstein, "Timeline for a Body: 4 Hours in the Middle of a Ferguson Street," *New York Times*, August 23, 2014. www.nytimes.com.
43. Barbara Ransby, *Making All Black Lives Matter: Reimagining Freedom in the Twenty-First Century*. Berkeley: University of California Press, 2018. Kindle edition.
44. Quoted in Josh Hafner, "How Michael Brown's Death, Two Years Ago, Pushed #BlackLivesMatter into a Movement," *USA Today*, August 8, 2016. www.usatoday.com.
45. Ben Miller, "Police Body Cameras: Digging Through the Data," *Government Technology*, January 1, 2019. www.govtech.com.
46. Patrick Oliver, "Creating a Multicultural Law Enforcement Agency: An Intentional Priority," *Police Chief Magazine*, March 2017. www.policechiefmagazine.org.
47. Quoted in Ariel Worthy, "Pittsburgh Wants to Hire More Black Officers, Some Say It Has to Change from Within," WITF, September 6, 2019. www.witf.org.
48. Quoted in *USA Today*, "'Starbucks Coffee is Anti-Black' Say Chanting Protesters at Philadelphia Starbucks Where 2 Black Men Were Arrested," April 16, 2018. www.usatoday.com.
49. Quoted in Starbucks.com, "Starbucks to Close All Stores Nationwide for Racial-Bias Education on May 29," April 17, 2018. https://stories.starbucks.com.

50. Quoted in Aaron Randle, "Racial Slurs, and the 15 Days That Shook Syracuse," *New York Times*, November 17, 2019. www.nytimes.com.

51. Quoted in Melanie Burney, "Gov. Murphy Signs Hair Discrimination Bill Inspired by South Jersey Wrestler Who Had His Dreadlocks Cut," *Philadelphia Inquirer*, December 19, 2019. www.inquirer.com.

52. Quoted in Burney, "Gov. Murphy."

53. Quoted in Bonny Scheltema, "Quan Neloms Is Actively Recruiting Black Men to Teach in Detroit's Public Schools," NBC News, October 16, 2019. www.nbcnews.com.

54. Quoted in Scheltema, "Quan Neloms."

**Black Lives Matter**—https://blacklivesmatter.com

Black Lives Matter organizes community action against violence inflicted against black citizens by police. The group also raises campaign funds for candidates dedicated to ending police violence against African Americans. The website includes a link to contact information for chapters found throughout the country.

**Campaign for Black Male Achievement**
www.blackmaleachievement.org

The New York City–based organization conducts programs to encourage black teens to finish school and begin productive careers. One program encourages successful black men to become mentors to urban teens. By accessing the "community" link on the group's website, visitors can see a city-by-city guide assessing how active African American men are in mentoring teens.

**Federal Bureau of Investigation**
www.fbi.gov/services/cjis/ucr/hate-crime

Maintained by the federal government's chief law enforcement agency, the website tracks hate crimes dating back to 1996. Hate crimes are offenses targeted at victims because of their race, faith, ethnicity, or gender preference. Visitors can find data on the crimes and victims by accessing the link for Hate Crime Statistics Annual Reports.

**Jim Crow Museum of Racist Memorabilia**
www.ferris.edu/jimcrow/what.htm

Maintained by Ferris State University in Michigan, the museum features exhibits highlighting the Jim Crow era in American history. Visitors to the museum's website can learn about the story of the white entertainer Thomas Dartmouth Rice and his creation of the buffoonish field slave character he named "Jim Crow."

**Mapping Police Violence**—https://mappingpoliceviolence.org

Organized by three data scientists, the website maintained by the group tracks police violence against black citizens. The website provides statistical data on police shootings, broken down by location of the shootings and ethnicities of the victims. Data highlighted by the website shows, for example, that many police shootings occur in communities with low crime rates.

**Southern Poverty Law Center**—www.splcenter.org

The Alabama-based organization monitors hate groups in America. The group has made copies of its publication *The Alt-Right on Campus: What Students Need to Know* available on its website. The guide helps college students identify alt-right propaganda and how to respond should a student be approached by an alt-right activist on campus.

# FOR FURTHER RESEARCH

## Books

Jennifer E. Cobbina, *Hands Up, Don't Shoot*. New York: New York University Press, 2019.

Henry Louis Gates Jr., *Stony the Road: Reconstruction, White Supremacy, and the Rise of Jim Crow*. New York: Penguin Books, 2019.

George Hawley, *The Alt-Right: What Everyone Needs to Know*. New York: Oxford University Press, 2018.

Ron Johnson, *13 Days in Ferguson*. Carol Stream, IL.: Tyndale Momentum, 2018.

Sean Wilentz, *No Property in Man: Slavery and Antislavery at the Nation's Founding*. Cambridge, MA: Harvard University Press, 2019.

## Internet Sources

Jeremy Bauer-Wolf, "White Supremacy Activity Spreads on Campuses," *Inside Higher Ed*, June 27, 2019. www.insidehighered.com.

Ken Belson, "Only Three NFL Head Coaches Are Black. 'It's Embarrassing,'" *New York Times*, December 31, 2019. www.nytimes.com.

Cassi Pittman Claytor, "'Shopping While Black': Yes, Bias Against Black Customers Is Real," *The Guardian* (Manchester, UK), June 24, 2019. www.theguardian.com.

Jailyn Gladney, "Boston University Is Proof That University Campuses Are Anything but 'Post-Racial,'" *The Nation* July 14, 2015. www.thenation.com.

Amina Kahn, "Getting Killed by Police Is a Leading Cause of Death for Young Black Men in America," *Los Angeles Times*, August 16, 2019. www.latimes.com.

Glenn C. Loury, "An American Tragedy: The Legacy of Slavery Lingers in Our Cities' Ghettos," Brookings Institution, March 1, 1998. www.brookings.edu.

Patrick Oliver, "Creating a Multicultural Law Enforcement Agency: An Intentional Priority," *Police Chief Magazine*, March 2017. www.policechiefmagazine.org.

Aaron Randle, "Racial Slurs, and the 15 Days That Shook Syracuse," *New York Times*, November 17, 2019. www.nytimes.com.

Bonny Scheltema, "Quan Neloms Is Actively Recruiting Black Men to Teach in Detroit's Public Schools," NBC News, October 16, 2019. www.nbcnews.com.

Jesse Washington, "The Untold Story of Wrestler Andrew Johnson's Dreadlocks," TheUndefeated.com, September 18, 2019. https://theundefeated.com.

# INDEX

# PICTURE CREDITS

# ABOUT THE AUTHOR

Hal Marcovitz is a former newspaper reporter and columnist who makes his home in Chalfont, Pennsylvania. He is the author of more than two hundred books for young readers.